HOPE beyond the STARS

An inspiring search for justice, truth & healing

Leeanne Truesdale

Copyright © 2023 Leeanne Truesdale
Print Edition

All rights reserved. No part of this book may be used or reproduced by any means, graphic, electronic, or mechanical, including photocopying, recording, taping or by any information storage retrieval system without the prior written permission of the author except in the case of articles and reviews permitted by copyright law.

Table of Contents

Foreword	v
1. Childhood	1
2. The Start of the Abuse	6
3. Teenage Years	17
4. Early Adulthood	25
5. Married Life	30
6. Downward Spiral Rock Bottom	39
7. Outside Intervention	44
8. Breakthrough in Recovery	49
9. Time to Face My Trauma	56
10. Pandora's Box	63
11. Surprise Flashback	66
12. Fighting for the Truth	74
13. Court Week	79
14. Turn of Events	84
15. Retribution	89
16. Acceptance	95
Final Words of Gratitude	97
Starlight	99
About the Author	103

Foreword

This is my truth.

For those of us who have experienced abuse, we can never forget what happened, but we can stop the memories creating more pain.

We are survivors. We can live the life that we want and, most importantly, deserve.

We are wounded healers. We can shine our light. We can be a lighthouse in the dark for others.

This is a story of hope, recovery and healing.

It is time to start my journey back.

CHAPTER ONE
Childhood

MY JOURNEY BEGAN the moment my life fell apart.

I imagined myself standing in the middle of a field surrounded by bricks with the smell of smouldering ash. The night sky was dark with a hint of angry red. Silence deafened me.

It felt like pain was seeping inside my skin and smothering me to my very core. I had tried to hide my pain for so long and now it was fighting back.

My world had fallen apart. Everything I knew, felt and experienced was just an illusion. The little girl inside me was stomping her feet and screaming: "I am not giving up! I want my voice to be heard! I want to be free!"

The little girl screamed until her tears ran dry and tiredness drained her.

With my Aunt and Uncle by my side, and the strength of my faith, this is my journey; from tears and sorrow, to healing and freedom.

The Truth shall prevail.

My earliest memories were when I was five years old. My Aunt Susan and Uncle Robert were due to be married and I was their flower girl. I got to wear a beautiful dress with a pair of ballet shoes. I felt so excited and special. The dress was white and bouncy and the shoes; I loved the shoes. They were also white with silk ribbon tied delicately around my ankles.

I felt so special, like a princess. A family member brought me up to dance at the evening party. I danced and danced.

That was the last time I remember feeling normal.

We moved house, not far from where we had been living. We settled in at number 34; two doors down from my grandmother's house. Mum got a new job working in a shop at the bottom of our estate.

Nan was the main provider of our family, holding us all together. My grandfather, Papa, died when I was two. Nan helped to feed us and made sure we had presents on Christmas morning.

My two brothers stayed with Nan a lot after Papa died. They weren't around much, so I spent a lot of time on my own, including summer holidays. I played with my dolls and sat with my cat Tiger. Tiger was very special to me; my rock. She never judged me, cuddling up to me in times of sadness. I loved her to the moon and back. I also loved playing outside on my roller skates. I was in my element when skating around the block.

I started primary school that year. On my

first day of school, mum brought me downstairs to put my uniform on. It was so cold in the house. I got dressed in front of the soft glow from the fireside. I was crying, not wanting to go to school. Looking back, I realise it was because I didn't like change of any sort.

I didn't like school much, but I made a friend in my class. Her name was Sarah and we ended up being best friends. I was quiet and kept myself to myself, unless I was with Sarah. We played and laughed together. Dependent on her, I clung to her and relied on her.

We met at the bottom of the hill every morning to walk to school together. When she was off sick or didn't show up, I had to walk to the school gates by myself, through the big playground which felt intimidating. Scared, paranoid and fearful, I didn't know what I was going to do at break and lunch time. How was I going to occupy myself? I wouldn't mingle with anyone else. I didn't know how to. I was shy and got embarrassed easily. I didn't like to stand out. So I just walked around or sat somewhere out of the way until the bell rang to go back in. This was the worst thing about primary school for me. I hated being alone but I didn't have the courage to mingle with other kids. When Sarah was in school with me, I felt safe and less fearful. It was like I didn't know how to be myself when I was alone.

One day, Sarah and I were sitting at our

desks in class when a new boy walked in. The moment I laid eyes on him, it felt as though my heart was jumping out of my chest. There was something familiar about him. It was as though I knew him already. He was slim, with short black hair and a cheeky smile. There was a hint of mischievousness about him. Instantly, I liked him. My cheeks blushed every time he walked past. He was the new kid on the block. Alan.

I fancied him like mad.

Alan sat beside me sometimes, which I loved. Of course, I didn't show it. He borrowed my colouring pencils, promising to return them, which he never did.

One day, Alan got scolded for being naughty and was sent to the back of the classroom as punishment. He called me over, asking to borrow a pencil. I'll never forget what happened that day. He kissed me on the lips.

I always had a soft spot for him. We ended up dating in secondary school, but as we grew older, we hung around with different kids and drifted apart.

However, I never forgot that moment at the back of the classroom. It will always stay with me.

He was kind, funny and loved to joke. Always smiling, he had a big heart. We were soul mates. Although we parted ways after school, we came back together in a whole different light. Little did I know, he would play a big part in my recovery and healing.

I don't have memories of many good times in childhood, other than the time spent with my cat and with my friend Sarah. There is one good memory that sticks out though and that is the comfort I got from my Plush Teddy; a pink elephant. I called her "Nelly" after the cartoon: "Nelly the Elephant." Dad brought her home for me one evening and because I doted on my dad, I cherished her. To this day, she still sits on my bed.

CHAPTER TWO
The Start of the Abuse

MY RELATIONSHIP WITH my mum was tainted for some time as a result of what happened to me as a child. However, when I was a child, I had my mum on a pedestal. I adored her. Dad was never really there.

Mum started working at the local shop and dad was a car mechanic. Dad wasn't able to spend much time with us as he was always working. If he wasn't working, he was in the pub. Mum and Dad argued quite a bit. Their marriage was toxic and I hated hearing them arguing. I used to put my fingers in my ears to try to block out the noise. I went to bed every night, praying they wouldn't argue.

People came and went from our house. Mum and Dad had friends over for drinks sometimes. On those nights, I was sent to bed. I used to keep my fingers in my ears until the shouting stopped. Sometimes I heard mum cry after dad walked out. My stomach hurt with anxiety so I curled up in a ball.

One day, my dad brought a new friend home. George lived two doors down from us. George worked with dad sometimes, helping him with cars. They also drank together occasionally.

George was tall and thin, with dark hair, big glasses and a pointy nose. His eyes were small, like pins. He wore jeans and a t-shirt and always looked untidy.

"Hello Lee," he said, introducing himself.

I was sitting on the grey sofa watching cartoons. I was 6 years old.

Looking up at him, I felt so small. He was tall and towering over me.

Sometimes Mum went out with her friends for drinks, so Dad stayed in with a few beers. I was always put to bed before mum went out and wasn't allowed downstairs until morning. Dad didn't interact with me much. Looking back, I think he actually didn't know how to.

If I needed a glass of water, I would creep downstairs quietly and gently knock on the door. I always felt like I was walking on eggshells.

My brothers got to stay up late, watching movies with Dad and eating Chinese takeaway, while I was sent to bed.

I used to sneak halfway down the stairs, listening to their muffled voices so I didn't feel alone. I was scared of the dark and felt so left out. As soon as I heard them moving, I crept back upstairs again.

Sometimes my brothers said: "Lee is listening at the door."

They shouted at me to get back to bed. It was a lonely time. I never understood why I was left out.

On one particular Friday evening, Mum went out and Dad stayed in. He got a few beers and George joined him for a drink. I walked to the kitchen for a glass of water. I was wearing my pink nightdress.

George looked at me and smiled. "Hello Lee."

Shyly, I replied, "Hi."

Dad said: "Go to bed, Lee."

I went to bed and lay there for ages, but I couldn't sleep. My room was small and pink. Lots of teddy bears sat on the floor. I covered them with blankets at night, worrying they would get cold. My bed was facing the door so I could see the hallway.

I remember lying on my back and hearing the living room door open. I listened to footsteps coming up the stairs. George appeared at the top of the stairs. He stopped and looked at me, then looked at the bathroom door. Instead of going to the toilet, he came into my room. He knelt down in front of my bed.

"You should be sleeping," he whispered. He chatted for a few minutes.

"Do you trust me?" he asked. "I am not going to hurt you."

I nodded. I had no reason not to trust him. He was my Dad's friend. I trusted my dad, so I trusted George.

He told me to open my legs.

I didn't have any knickers on. Mum always

said: "you need to let the air at you at night".

He started to touch my private parts.

"Does this feel nice?"

I froze in confusion. I couldn't understand what he was doing. I couldn't answer; I could only nod my head in agreement. The next few moments were a blur.

When he was finished, he got up. He told me that I was his friend now and we were to keep this a secret. I wasn't to tell my mum, dad or anyone. He said that if I told anyone, something bad would happen to mum and dad. It would all be my fault.

His tone of voice was calm, quiet and controlled.

He walked out of my room and went back downstairs. I turned over on my side, legs tucked under me, wondering what had just happened.

I believe my brain blocked that experience out because when I woke the next morning, I felt nothing.

It wasn't until sometime later that it came back to me.

I don't know how much time had passed, but it hit me like a bus. I was getting out of the bath. Mum had gone downstairs, leaving me to get dried.

Going into my bedroom, all of a sudden, a sickening feeling gripped my stomach. It was so intense that it knocked me sideways onto my bed. I curled up into a ball, clutching my stomach and squeezing it. I wanted to scream, but I couldn't get any sound out. Getting back up, I lifted my hairdryer and started hitting it against my head. It was as if I was trying to knock the memory out of my head.

From that day on, I was never the same.

George instilled so much fear in me that it prevented me from bonding with anyone. He knew I adored my mum and dad, so he used that to threaten me. He told me that no one would ever believe me and if I ever told anyone, he would kill my parents. That was enough to shut me up.

He also manipulated me into feeling sorry for him. He said that his wife had died and he felt so alone. He told me I was special and made him happy. I was trapped. I feared for my mum and dad's safety, going to bed every night praying they'd come home safely. George continued to sexually abuse me at any given opportunity.

George knew how to manipulate people and he could see I was vulnerable. Dad was never there, always out at work. Mum was either working or drinking with friends, stuck in her own world, forgetting about my needs. Looking back, I can see she did her best, but she was so wrapped up in herself, she couldn't hear me.

I felt so alone as a little girl. When the abuse started, I retreated into myself. During the summer holidays, I was stuck to my mum's heels. I didn't have anyone to play with in my area, especially kids my own age.

Mum told me to go out to the garden and play. I didn't have anything to do. It was years later before I got a pair of roller boots. I went to the front garden and sat in the little square of grass that was surrounded by small hedges. Tiger lay beside me. I sat on the greenery, playing with a blade of grass. That memory has stuck with me. I was alone and sad, with nothing to play with other than a blade of grass.

My Nan wandered past. "Cheer up love! What's wrong? Why don't you do something instead of just sitting there?"

I couldn't put it into words because I didn't even know what was wrong.

"I don't know what's wrong," I replied, shrugging my shoulders.

If Dad was working, Mum made me tag along when she went drinking at her friend's house. Sometimes, we weren't getting back home until sunrise. It was exhausting, being up half the night while mum got drunk, laughed, cried and fell into a stupor.

After a while, mum stopped taking me to her friend's house and George began babysitting me.

I dreaded the weekend. When mum announced that she was heading out and George would be minding me, I cried and asked her not to go.

But she ignored my pleas every time.

I saw George walking up the hill with his blue bag of beers in hand. I felt sick. Panic took over me. I would have no way of escaping him. I cried: "Mum, please don't go out, please!"

But she never listened. She didn't even ask why.

Mum put me to bed and I curled up in a ball. I heard the front door close behind her.

"Lee, come downstairs."

I entered the living room, my nightie on. George pulled his jeans down to his knees. He told me to come over to him and took my hand.

"Pretend it's a lollipop."

Afterwards, I felt confused and dirty. Sheer panic made me feel like my head was going to explode.

On other occasions, he crawled into bed beside me.

Just when I was about to doze off, I felt him creep in behind me, his breath in my ear, stinking of alcohol and cigarettes.

"Please no!" I screamed silently in my head. When he parted my legs, my body went numb. It was as though I had floated outside of my body, into the top corner of the room.

On another occasion, Mum had a Christmas party in our house, inviting all the staff from the shop. Alcohol bottles lined the worktops and people were hanging around the kitchen, topping up their drinks.

Dad and George arrived. George got a beer and sat at the kitchen dining table, while Dad went into the living room.

I was standing there in my nightie with my blanket in my arms.

George was glaring at me.

He told me to come over and sit on his knee.

The look on his face sparked so much fear in me that I did what I was told.

When I sat on his knee, he draped the blanket over me. He proceeded to touch me under the blanket, in the middle of the party. No-one noticed. They were all drunk; laughing and dancing.

At one stage, I did try to challenge George. When he came into my room one night, I was sitting with my legs crossed on my bed.

Mustering all my courage, I threatened: "I'm going to tell Mum and Dad what you're doing!"

But he still managed to shut me up.

So I did try.

Unless you're in that position, you can't possibly imagine the fear that goes on in a child's mind.

There was one of the times that George touched me which was a bit different to the others.

My cousin had come up to stay at my Nan's house one weekend. We were a similar age and had so much fun together. Colouring in at my Nan's kitchen table, I loved his company. We could be silly and laugh about everything.

One day, we were at home and Mum and

Dad were out. I think Dad had gone to deliver a car to a customer and mum was at work. Nan was keeping an eye on us.

George walked into the house and asked: "Where is your Dad, Lee?"

"Delivering a car, I think," I replied.

Then George asked me and my cousin to go into the store room. There was coal for the fire in there, along with other bits and bobs like the hoover. George sat on some boxes. He asked us if we would like to play a game.

He asked us to take off our clothes and touch each other.

That feeling of dirtiness returned.

I remember my cousin's look of shock.

Nan arrived out of nowhere and before we had the chance to remove any clothing, she told George to leave.

I don't know if Nan realised what was about to happen, but I'm forever grateful.

It seems George wanted to take an even greater risk by involving my cousin but thankfully, he didn't get the chance.

After that incident, my cousin stopped coming to stay at Nan's at the weekends. I asked mum why he wasn't coming. She shouted, hysterically in tears: "Get to your bedroom, he's not coming and that's that."

I remember feeling so alone and scared. My tummy was sick with fear. I felt so trapped. I didn't have the relief of my cousin being there to give me a welcome distraction. Even that was gone now.

You would think that the abuse would have stopped after that, but it didn't. For whatever reason, George continued to abuse me.

I was so confused that I didn't get to see my cousin any more. I had no idea mum was told about the incident with me and my cousin.

I was consumed with fear and panic every day. There was no rest. I couldn't understand why I felt the way I felt. At times I couldn't eat. I woke in the middle of the night, sweating after horrific nightmares. I felt like I was losing my mind. The sensation of nausea and panic plagued me.

Unfortunately for me, my troubles were about to get worse. It was only the start of a very long road.

The physical pain had stopped, but the mental and emotional pain persisted. I didn't know what was wrong with me.

George eventually stopped abusing me when I turned 9 years old. When the abuse stopped, thoughts plagued me which were negative, yet bizarre.

"Why isn't George bothering with me anymore? What's wrong with me?"

As much as I was relieved it had ended, I was left with the aftermath of emotional damage. I told myself over and over that I needed to forget what happened. However, the feelings of fear and panic stayed with me. Added to this, I also felt dirty, yet I didn't know why. I used to walk around the block every night, burning off energy, praying for the bad dreams to stop. "Please don't let me have any nightmares tonight, please," I begged, over and over.

Later on in adulthood, I found out I was suffering from CPTSD. Due to it never being treated, this condition only got worse as time went on.

I felt so sad. Inside, I was screaming for someone to tell me I was going to be okay. I felt like I was invisible. I felt numb. It was my wee cat Tiger that gave me comfort.

She was my rock during those days. When I lifted her up, she put her paws around my neck and gave me little head-bumps. She waited at the bottom of the drive for me coming home from school. Every day, without fail, she was there. She also lay on top of me at night, never leaving my side.

I had Tiger for a long time.

It devastated me when she went missing. One morning, she went out and never came home. I stood at the door every night calling for her for months. She never showed up. I cried myself to sleep for months, but I never gave up hope of her coming back to me.

CHAPTER THREE
Teenage Years

SOME PEOPLE HAVE asked me: "Why didn't you tell anyone?"

I believe in my own way, I did try. When I was around 10, I told a boy who fancied me. Ryan and I lived near each other and went to the same school. He was always asking me out. We were playing outside one day and he asked me to go to his room so we could be alone. I followed him.

A part of me wanted to be with him, but panic hit when he asked to kiss me.

I couldn't bring myself to do it, but at the same time I didn't want to let him down. I didn't know how to say no.

Instead, I told him I couldn't kiss him because George had been touching me.

I think there was a part of me asking for help by confiding this big secret.

Ryan called me a "fridget".

Looking back, perhaps he couldn't comprehend the magnitude of my secret.

When he called me a "fridget", I didn't understand what he meant, but it felt like I'd done something wrong. The feeling of dirtiness returned.

Eventually my mum and dad split up. Mum met a new partner and we moved from our house at No. 34 to our new home just across the footpath.

It felt like the start of a new beginning.

However, feelings of panic still haunted me. I tried to convince myself to forget what happened. I turned it over and over in my mind, trying to push it away.

My wish was granted.

I know now that I chose to blank it out and dissociate myself from the abuse. However, the nasty feelings didn't go away. Unknowingly, I numbed them out. My coping mechanism was to deny my emotions.

As my time at primary school came to an end, I developed an issue with my left leg. I had been having trouble with it for months before mum and dad finally took me to the doctors. I had been running in a school race one day and fell over. A sharp pain shot to my left hip as I scrambled off the grass. As well as a limp, I was also in considerable pain, which I just tried to ignore. That was until the pain got really bad.

The doctor said I had growing pains and it was nothing to worry about.

I was left in pain for a while longer until eventually, my leg seized up. I was walking with my leg sticking out to the side. I could no longer bend it or align it with my other leg. In constant agony and tears, I couldn't even bend down to put on my socks or shoes. Mum had to help me get dressed in the mornings.

Eventually, Mum took me back to the doctors. It was during the summer holidays before I was about to start High School and just a couple of days before my birthday. The doctor examined my leg and told me I had to go to hospital immediately. My hip joint had come away from my hip socket.

I really wanted to spend my birthday at home, so the doctor agreed I could go into hospital the day after my birthday. I was 10 years old.

It turned out that I had a SCAFE (Slipped Capital Femoral Epiphysis). I don't remember much about hospital apart from the fact that I couldn't sleep and I had a weight fitted to my left leg. I was confined to bed at all times. There was a long plaster which ran along both sides of my leg. At the bottom of the plaster, there was a weight pulling my leg. This was to hold my hip joint in place. I was positioned like this for four weeks solid.

If it failed to work, they said I'd need surgery where they would have to fit a pin into my hip. The thought of surgery terrified me.

Graham, the boy in the bed opposite me, had the same thing and he had to have surgery. Graham was nice. His family also chatted away to me. I got on well with his sister and we vowed to keep in touch.

The doctors noticed I wasn't eating the hospital food. They threatened that if I didn't start eating, they wouldn't let me go home.

The doctor instructed I've have to learn to walk with crutches before I left hospital. I would have to use them for a year.

As I was about to start High School, I was given the option to take a year out to recover, but I insisted I wanted to start in September. I suppose I didn't want to be left behind.

When I got home from hospital, I had enough time to get used to the crutches.

The first day of school was nerve-wrecking. It was bad enough that I was shy and didn't like anyone looking at me, but I had crutches which made me stand out even more. We had to go to Assembly to register and be appointed to our teachers. I was slower than everyone else. With the clicking of my crutches excruciatingly loud, I hobbled into the Assembly Hall, my cheeks red as crimson.

All the first years had to go up to the front of the hall and stand near the stage. Regardless of how embarrassed I felt, I hobbled to the front amid all the stares. Awkwardly, I sat down as I had been told not to put any pressure on my leg under any circumstances.

I was also exempt from P.E. that year, which was brilliant. I wasn't into sport anyway.

I managed to make a friend called Charlene who I hung around with in school and sometimes after school. She lived on the street next to mine. Charlene and I were close, laughing together and being a support to each another.

Going through first year of school, I buried the abuse to the back of my mind. I was more interested in being a typical teenager; hanging out with Charlene and listening to music. We talked about our favourite bands and about the boys we fancied in class. Of course, I still fancied Alan, but there were a couple of other boys who I also liked.

My sexual side was awake and had been since the abuse first happened, but those feelings scared me. I didn't understand what was happening to me.

I was so self-conscious and a couple of girls had started to bully me in school. They took my crutches at lunchtime. I was left standing against the wall, holding myself up until the bullies gave the crutches back.

Extremely shy, I could never defend myself. My two brothers (who went to the same school) never stood up for me either.

I always wore my hair up in a ponytail as my hair was so thick and annoying. The bullies pulled my ponytail. It used to annoy me so much, but I couldn't fight back.

Until one day when I was older.

In fourth year, one of the bullies, Christine, sat behind me in class. When the teacher popped out of the classroom, Christine took the opportunity to taunt me.

Rage rose up within me.

I stood up, grabbed my chair and threw it at her.

Of course, I got into trouble with the

teacher. My punishment was not getting my lunch break. I hated getting into trouble over that. I turned the anger inwards to myself, blaming myself.

From then on, I vowed to keep myself to myself. I sat in the cloakrooms at break-times and lunch. Charlene was happy to sit with me. She didn't have a great time in school either. Playing at home was no different. I was scared to go outside in case the bullies would see me. I was on high-alert all the time.

I was still having nightmares and that dreadful feeling of fear and panic came up on a regular basis. Not knowing what was happening to me, I continued to suffer. I was really dependent on my friend Charlene. We had a lot of fun, but as time went on, I started to hang out with other kids who lived nearby.

A few of them were older than me and I seemed to be drawn to them. Before I knew it, I was drinking alcohol and smoking behind the local swimming pool. There was a run-down deserted garage where the local alcoholics would drink. This became my hangout with the other kids. We would scrape money together to buy beer and cigarettes, then spent the weekend drinking and smoking. Although I joined in with the crowd, I still was quite naïve and innocent. I didn't drink too much as I knew I had to go home and I didn't want mum smelling the booze.

I got to know one of the alcoholics. His name was Bopper. He rode a bicycle everywhere. He was quiet and had a lot of knowledge and wisdom. I grew to like Bopper. He was funny and told us stories. We would laugh and sing songs. He took me under his wing while I was hanging out at the deserted garage. I was 15 years old at the time. Bopper used to say: "Leeanne, you don't belong down here."

In hindsight, I think he spotted my addictive personality and was trying to warn me away from alcohol.

I knew he had a drink problem but I had no idea how serious his alcoholism was, until a few years later, when he died from the disease.

I met another guy at the hangout. He was also an alcoholic although I didn't think much of it at that time. I guess I was pretty naive. He asked me out and we started dating, which was a disaster from the start. Mum and Dad knew about Jason's drinking and the bad company he kept. They didn't want me to date him and did everything they could to keep me away from him, but I kept going back to him. I was besotted.

After many arguments with my parents, Dad told me I had to end the relationship or he would disown me. I fought against my family and chose to stay in the relationship. My dad wasn't pleased, but he just distanced himself and let me get on with it.

Eventually though, at the age of seventeen, I finished it with Jason. Deep down, I knew he was bad news. I stopped going to the hangout and subsequently left the old acquaintances behind. Swallowing my pride, I approached my dad to see if he was still annoyed with me. Relieved I had ended the relationship, he just said, "Let's just forget about it and move on". Thankfully, my relationship with my Dad was back on track.

After that, I found myself on my own. I had no friends. Everyone was disappearing. I remember thinking: "Why don't I have genuine friends? Why can't I keep people in my life?"

I really felt like there was something wrong with me. That's the only way I could describe it. I was just "wrong". At one point, I thought I was going crazy. Was I too much for people? Was I stupid? Was I not worthy enough to be part of life?

I fell into a deep depression. Panic and anxiety took over. The feeling of dirtiness was getting stronger and stronger. Mum noticed I wasn't right. She told me to go to the doctors which I did. I couldn't articulate what I was feeling other than depressed. The doctor prescribed anti-depressants.

I was, and still am, a loner in many ways. I have two friends who I can trust now as an adult. Through my faith in my higher power, I have come to understand that this was how it was meant to be for me; to travel through life by myself.

CHAPTER FOUR
Early Adulthood

MY LAST DAY of school was terrifying. I had no idea what I wanted to do. I loved art but that was it. Dad told me I had to go out, get a job and earn money.

My GCSE results were awful so I enrolled on an administration course in our local college. The course ran for one year and would help me to gain a qualification. It was good experience and by the end of it, I started working in an office environment.

I experienced my first Christmas office party, which was quite strange as it was a lot more glamorous than hanging out at a run-down garage. I loved the feeling of being part of something. I was still shy but I joined in the best I could. I found adulthood to be both exciting and scary at the same time.

I believe nobody is prepared for adult life. I certainly wasn't.

I navigated my way through employment and a year later, decided to move to a different job. I met different people and partied with colleagues after work on Friday. I still lived with my mum and stepdad and I had boyfriends on and off.

Eventually, I met my long term boyfriend at a pub one night where he worked as a barman. I was nineteen at the time and Ross was twelve years older than me. He was very influential, and I was easily influenced. We partied hard and moved in with each other about a year into the relationship. Things were good for a while and then I felt like my life was restricted. He became very possessive, always needing to know where I was, who I was talking to and who was texting me. He took me to work and picked me up. I didn't realise it at the time but our relationship was very toxic. I wasn't allowed to go out with my friends, who eventually stopped asking me. I didn't go to work events either as it was too much hassle to explain why I wanted to go. If I was lucky enough to go out with my brother, Ross made sure he picked me up. Eventually, I stopped going out.

It felt like life was passing me by.

When Ross was working at a pizza delivery shop, I had to go with him. He didn't want me sitting in the house while he wasn't there. Weekend after weekend, I felt more and more isolated.

When anyone came to see us, he was always in a bad mood or didn't make them feel welcome. So eventually, my family stopped visiting too.

It got to the point where we were always arguing and I never had my own space. My self-esteem was very low and I was drinking a lot.

My brother had invited Ross to a motorbike show which was held every year in May. It was supposed to be a lads' weekend but Ross insisted I go too, otherwise he wouldn't go.

So on the Friday, we set off to Portrush. We rode all the way there on his motorbike which was a long time for me to be sitting on the back of his bike. I tried to enjoy the weekend as much as I could, but it was all about drinking beer and sleeping in a tent.

By this stage of our relationship, I was so unhappy but I didn't know how to get out of it. My brother had invited a few of his friends to the show also. Although it was a welcome break from the norm, I had to be really careful what I said. I would get the brunt of Ross's jealousy when no-one was around.

One of my brother's friends seemed really nice and kind. I did fancy him and we caught each other's eye all weekend.

The journey home was horrendous. Not only was I hung-over, but I felt so alone and emotionally numb. I wanted to cry out for help but I couldn't.

While speeding down the motorway, the thought occurred to me that I could just let go. It would end the pain I was feeling inside.

Manipulative and jealous, I felt suffocated by Ross. He controlled every part of my life. Looking back, I gave my power away to someone who was always putting me down physically, emotionally and mentally. I couldn't find my voice.

The guy I fancied was called Clive. I wasn't aware at the time, but he had given his mobile number to my brother, asking him to pass it on should I ever become single.

Later on, he was to become my husband.

The day after Portrush, I knew I had to leave Ross.

When he went to work, I called in sick and packed up as much clothes and shoes as I could. I walked away from all my other belongings. I called my brother Chris, asking him to come down and help me move out. Chris was very good to me. I adored him and we were always close. He didn't like the way my boyfriend treated me.

I left the house that day and never returned.

Ross tried to win me back on several occasions, but I knew it was over.

Eventually I had to let the house go and he kept everything. We had bought a lot of stuff for our home on loan. He hadn't been able to get credit so the loans were all in my name. I had five credit cards at one stage.

Eventually, he stopped paying his fair share and left me with all the debt. I struggled to make ends meet, which caused a lot of stress and impacted my mental health. The depression returned although thankfully the drinking wasn't as bad.

Dad stepped in to help. He took me to a professional who helped me combine my debts into one affordable payment each month.

It was around this time that I got in contact with Clive using the mobile number he had passed on. I knew there was something between us. Even though I was going through a lot of stress, Clive and I met up a few times and started dating. Despite my financial situation, he chose to stay with me. He really stepped up to support me and to this day I am forever grateful.

CHAPTER FIVE
Married Life

IT TOOK TIME to cut the dead ends of that relationship out of my life, but I felt a weight fall off my shoulders when I started dating Clive. We were a happy couple. Finally, I felt content.

I stayed at his house every weekend but missed him terribly during the week when I had to go back to mum's house and my normal work routine.

I counted my lucky stars for meeting Clive. I thought I'd never find anybody who would make me as happy as he did.

"Is this actually happening to me?" I thought. I couldn't quite believe it. Part of me felt like it was all a dream. Someone like me didn't deserve to be in a happy relationship, I told myself.

Eight months into our relationship, Clive took me to a beautiful hotel. In our hotel room, he got down on one knee and proposed. Of course, I said yes. We had a beautiful dinner that evening and it was a perfect night.

Although happy, there was still a distinct feeling of emptiness within, but I pushed that feeling aside. A year later, we were married on the 2nd June 2006. We had just bought a house in the country near his mum and dad's.

For the first two years of marriage, life was bliss. Clive worked hard, as did I. At weekends, we spent our time fixing things around the house and sometimes had friends over for dinner and drinks. We had two horses called Rab and Cindy. Rab (after Rab C. Nesbitt), was a pure white Connemara. Cindy was a Chestnut thoroughbred horse with a pure blonde mane and tail. We would take Rab out hacking at the weekends. Cindy, who had unfortunately been badly treated by her previous owner, was content to just graze in the fields. I took a shine to her, talking to her while I brushed her hair. I detected the hurt in her eyes and identified empathically with her.

Looking back, that part of my life was the happiest I've ever been; Clive, me, the horses and our collection of animals. I really didn't appreciate it enough at the time.

There was 'Mindy' the cat, who was grumpy when we first took her in, probably because she wasn't wanted by her previous owner. There was 'Darky', a small black Labrador, who went out with Clive when he was shooting birds. We had Siberian Huskies 'Sapphire' and 'Keira'. Sapphire was light grey with a white chest. She had beautiful piercing blue eyes and bounced around like a playful eejit. Keira was a rescue who had been mistreated. Timid with a touchy side, we were mindful of her sensitivities. She was pure ginger mixed with white fur.

When the pets were casting, the house would be covered with fur so we ended up brushing them outside in the garden. You would have thought we were shearing sheep.

Clive was very good with his hands and made a sleigh on wheels. We took the huskies out, with Clive standing on the back while the girls pulled him along the back roads. I was into keeping fit so I ran beside them. We bumped into the occasional farmer along the way.

As time went on, although all was well, I started to drink a bit more than normal.

I didn't think anything of it, but Clive noticed. Sometimes he would say: "Should we give the wine a break this weekend?"

I hated when he said that.

He was never a big drinker, but I always twisted his arm to share a bottle.

Things started to go downhill.

On the weekends, I was sleeping in later and later. When I did wake, it was with headaches and nausea.

There were many times when I didn't remember the night before. Clive had to fill me in on what I had done or said. Often times, I'd discover with shame that I had been verbally abusive to him and fallen all around the place.

When we went out at nights, I never wanted the party to end.

I should have noticed the slippery slope I

was sliding down, but I was in denial.

I loved how alcohol changed my personality. It made me feel confident and alive, although, it was short lived because the next morning, I paid the price.

It was a vicious circle I kept repeating over and over.

I went from drinking every weekend to drinking during the week after work.

"Just to relax," I said. "I deserve it after the day I've had."

In my mind, it was my reward. After all, I went to work, I kept the house tidy and tried to be a good wife. All the while, my insides churned with the craving for alcohol.

Sometimes I went to the pub after work, stayed for one too many and arrived home late. There were times I even fell asleep on the bus and ended up in a different town. I'd have to phone Clive and ask him to come and get me.

There was one night I didn't arrive home at all.

I had texted Clive to let him know I'd be getting the next bus home. But I woke up the following morning in my colleague's apartment. I asked him what happened the night before. He told me I was completely out of it. I couldn't even stand up so he had brought me back to his place. When I went into his bathroom, I apparently passed out. I had gone completely grey and he thought I was dead.

A vague memory came into my mind. I

remembered walking into the bathroom and feeling as though I was hallucinating. Lots of colours and weird shapes had danced before my eyes. Then, nothing.

I thanked him for looking after me, then phoned Clive, drumming up an excuse. I told him that I missed the bus so my friend let her stay at hers.

Walking down the road to the bus stop that morning, I felt so dirty and scared. I was clearly getting out of control and didn't understand how I had gone into a blackout.

I discussed it later with my colleague, retracing my steps and trying to piece the night together. I remembered going into the bar and standing with five other people. It was happy hour and I had ordered two pints for the price of one. That's all I could remember; after that, it was 'lights out'.

My colleague did a bit of digging. Apparently someone we worked with had spiked my drink for a laugh. He couldn't tell me who it was so I didn't push it. I got the impression he was warned not to say.

The paranoia was awful after that. When I had to walk past the sales guys in the office, I was convinced people were talking about me.

My only way to deal with it was to bury the experience deep within. I didn't report it to the police. I had thought about it, but I told myself no-one would believe me.

It was just another shameful self-inflicted act to add to the list.

I didn't even tell my husband.

It felt like I was slipping, as though my life was spiralling out of control. It terrified me, but I painted a smile on my face and said nothing.

Not long after, I fell pregnant. I managed to curtail my drinking during the pregnancy but I didn't stop drinking entirely. When I got to about six months though, my body rejected the alcohol. Sometimes I think it was probably my baby Eva rejecting the alcohol, which makes me smile.

I left work, taking a year out to concentrate on my daughter. Besides, they had asked if I wanted to take my maternity leave early. To be honest, I think the Managing Director wanted rid of me. I said yes. I was struggling with working in an office environment anyway.

When Eva was born, I remember looking down at her perfect little face and thinking: "Leeanne, you have a responsibility now. This little girl needs you."

The day Clive picked us up from the hospital was both exciting and daunting, for both of us.

At the start, I promised I wouldn't drink and would do my best to be a good mother.

However, on my first night out after the pregnancy, I took a drink and passed out in the toilets of our local pub. With not drinking alcohol for a few months, I guess my tolerance was on the floor.

When the drink was in, I argued with Clive, picking at him. Looking back, he really had the patience of a saint. He deserved a medal.

He had taken to marking the wine bottles behind my back, to work out if I'd been drinking. I had, but I had sipped the wine and then topped the bottle up with water.

It was selfish at the time, but I considered leaving Clive on several occasions. I told myself that he'd be happier without me; that I felt trapped by him. One day, I packed my bags, lifted Eva and left home.

The image of him sitting there in the living-room; in the dark, on his own, will haunt me for the rest of my life. It's a memory that is imprinted on my mind.

I drove to my mum's house, which was the beginning of my life rolling downhill at a rapid pace into the wall.

Clive was a good husband who loved me. He was, and still is, a good, hard-working country man with amazing values and morals, not to mention a good father. He is a man of honour who supported his family.

I still regret the decision to leave him. I don't think that will ever change. I was horrible to him. I drank and cheated; something that is actually so out of character for me. But when the drink was in, all sense went out the window. The guilt and shame that followed became a remorseful backpack, the burden heavier and heavier.

I didn't know who I was anymore. I had gone from an innocent child to a wreck; a liar and a cheat. It was as though I was in self-destruct mode, descending rapidly.

Someone told me once that I was a "car crash waiting to happen." Boy, were they right.

It wasn't until years later I realised that I had subconsciously sabotaged my marriage. Deep down, I believed I didn't deserve a good man.

The pain, anger and shame attached to my childhood slowly unravelled during the years I'd been married. I felt I wasn't worthy of receiving love. Clive really tried with me but I completely shut him out. The one person who showed me unconditional love was the person I pushed away. I'm not sure I'll ever forgive myself for depriving him and my daughter of a safe family unit.

A year and a half later, I asked Clive if he would like to get back together again. But by that time, he had moved on and found someone else; a woman he is still with today. I am happy for them. My daughter has gained a brother and sister who are amazing. She has siblings who will always be in her life. She has a safe family home in the country and I'm so proud of her. I'm glad that she has the support of, not only me, but her father and his family.

Opening up that suitcase of memories is one that still sits heavy on my heart. I've carried that baggage around for some time and it still aches when I think of this chapter of my life. If I could go back and change things I would, but unfortunately my complex past made me push away the one person who loved me.

I hope that one day I get the opportunity to tell him how sorry I am for hurting him. He will always have a place in my heart.

However, now I have to find a way of forgiving myself. That's the journey I need to travel so that one day, I can find love again.

CHAPTER SIX
Downward Spiral Rock Bottom

AFTER LEAVING MY husband, I stayed with my mum and stepdad for a while. They helped with Eva. Part of me loved being back home because they looked after me. It was as if I simply handed my responsibility back to them. Although I was living there with my daughter, I started drinking every night. As lovely as it was being looked after, I also really needed my own space.

Eventually, Eva and I moved into our own place. As usual, I vowed to cut back on the drinking. It worked for a while until the feeling of emptiness became too much and I'd pick up again.

The responsibility of being a mum weighed heavy on me. I really struggled with parenthood, especially the emotional side of things. I felt numb, as though there was nothing inside. I tried my best and cared for my daughter as much as I could. I fed her, clothed her and took her to the park. I even took her to the baby and toddler day centre when I could afford it. But when Eva went to bed at night, I'd open a bottle of wine. The occasional night turned into every night. When she went to her daddy's at the weekend, I spent the whole time drinking. Once the drink was in, I was rendered to the sofa. I have to say, being a parent and having a hangover is the worst combination.

Fridays and Saturdays were spent getting drunk by myself at home. I'd wake the following morning with no memory of the night before. Trying to locate my mobile phone, I'd walk into the kitchen to find empty bottles strewn along the counter.

At the time, I was still in denial about my drinking. My mum and stepdad would make comments about my alcohol intake but I brushed it off. Instead, I continued to do the same thing over and over, having the same results.

Lack of money became an issue, so my solution was to buy cheaper alcohol. Running out of drink made me feel panicky and fearful. I had to make sure I always had a stash. My solution: eat less, so I could drink more.

I could actually go without a drink for a couple of weeks if I was lucky. But then I'd hit the drink again with a vengeance. A binge drinker; that was me.

Most of the time, I felt numb. When there was an inkling of any uncomfortable emotions rising within me, I would drink. The periods between binges were getting shorter and shorter. My physical and mental health suffered greatly. Every time I drank, I blacked out. When the alcohol wore off, the shakes kicked in.

I was a nuisance, ringing and texting people at all hours of the night. My life revolved around lying on the sofa watching any drama or soap, anything to escape my mind.

Eventually, it got to the stage where the alcohol stopped working. It no longer blocked anything out. My tolerance must have gotten so high that it failed to have an effect.

It was at that point, I felt really low. I could actually feel myself slipping away from life. I knew I was killing myself but I couldn't stop.

There were many nights that I lay on the sofa, drinking and passing out. Sometimes I woke up to find the house in darkness with no electricity left in the meter. One time I woke up on the floor, red wine spilled all over the place with splatters of red up the walls. I must have drunk so much that I collapsed.

Whilst sitting on that sofa drinking, I used to look at the photo of my daughter on the fireplace. Her little face stared back at me. I willed myself to get sober for her, but the drink overpowered me every time. Instead, I just sat there, crying and feeling empty. I trailed my mattress into my daughter's room just so I could feel close to her. Even though she wasn't there, somehow it made me feel near her.

It got to the stage where I ended up drinking wine straight from the bottle. I fell asleep, only to wake up and repeat, for days on end. Thoughts of self-harm and suicide plagued me.

There was one evening when the drink was in and I took a knife to my arm, cutting it in anger. Blood was all over the kitchen floor and I ended up in A&E. They bandaged me up and I still bear the scar today. Suicidal thoughts were forefront in my mind. I just wanted the pain to stop.

One afternoon I drank all the alcohol left in the house. "I may as well end it now," I told myself. Finding all the tablets I could get my hands on, I swallowed them all and passed out. Apparently I had fallen down the stairs.

I woke to a loud banging on my front door. Somehow managing to get up, I staggered to the door. A friend had called to see me. I couldn't string two sentences together so he put me to bed. He stayed with me until the following morning to keep an eye on me.

It wasn't until years later that he found out I'd taken so many tablets that night.

I remember waking that night, my stomach cramping horrifically. I crawled to the bathroom, hanging over the toilet bowl to vomit. Worn out, I ended up lying on the bathroom floor.

I'm convinced that if I hadn't vomited that night, I wouldn't be here today.

There was one particularly bad drinking binge that went on for twelve days straight.

My stepdad came to visit, pleading with me to get help. Crying, I fell to my knees, sobbing: "please help me, please help me."

In fact, that was to be my last big session. After that binge, the withdrawals kicked in. With shaky legs, I couldn't stand. I had to crawl to the bathroom on my hands and knees. The hallucinations were so horrific and the comedown so debilitating that the doctor had to give me tablets to prevent seizures. An appropriate adult was needed to administer these to me over a five day period.

It was this pain and mental torture that made me finally hit my rock bottom. I knew, deep down, I was an alcoholic. I made the decision to go to Alcoholics Anonymous.

This was my first step to recovery.

CHAPTER SEVEN
Outside Intervention

MY FIRST NIGHT at AA was somewhat daunting, although I felt identification and comfort when I heard people sharing their stories. I continued to go back.

Despite the meetings, I still had cravings for alcohol and it wasn't long before I ended up hitting the drink again. This time, it was much worse. By then, I had a head full of AA and a belly full of drink. The guilt was horrible, not to mention the fear of losing my daughter.

I went back to AA with my tail between my legs, but the one thing I'm proud of is that I kept going back. Every time I took a drink, I picked myself up and tried again. It was like a revolving door. Every time I thought I'd hit my rock-bottom, there seemed to be another trap door and I fell even harder.

I phoned another AA member who was also struggling to stay sober. We ended up relapsing together. I remember standing in that bar looking around me. It felt like I was out of my body, frozen in time, observing the scene from afar. Everyone around me was smiling, laughing and having fun. Although physically drunk, my head felt as sober as a judge.

I stayed at her house that night and arrived back home the following morning, a bottle of Gin in my bag. Getting into bed, I dozed for a while and when I woke, the unopened bottle of Gin was sitting there, looking at me.

"I can't do this anymore," I told myself. "I'm done."

That was my moment of surrender.

"The actions you choose in a moment's thought can determine your fate."

Once more, I returned to AA, but this time I really started to listen.

Meanwhile, the Social Services came knocking at my door. My brother and his wife had decided to contact the Social Services.

Social Services arranged for my daughter to move out for six months and live under the care of my mother. They said that this was to keep her safe and to give me time to get help. I was allowed to stay overnight at mum's and see her; I just wasn't allowed to keep her at home as that was my drinking danger zone.

After I had dropped my daughter to school one morning, I arrived back to my mum's house. She showed me her laptop. "Lee, you need to see this…"

My brother and his wife had plastered a post all over social media about my drinking problem. They called me a "waste of space" and an unfit mother. They exposed me completely, dragging my daughter's name into it too. They tagged everyone – my family, my friends, my ex-husband Clive and all his family and friends.

It was then that my entire family found out about my issues. I couldn't believe what I was reading. People I didn't even know were writing horrible things about me. One person said I should be removed from society. I already hated myself, but when I read their comments, I felt lower than a snake's belly.

Despite all the hatred, Clive was the one who stood by me. He knew what my brother and his wife were like. He was appalled by all the trolls on social media.

I burst out crying to my mum. "What more do they want from me? I'm trying to sort my life out!" I had nothing left to give.

All I could do was continue to go to AA. In the AA meetings, I talked about it, cried and got it all out.

A feeling of hopelessness swamped me and suicidal thoughts were all-consuming. I became so desperate that one night I found myself falling to my knees, praying to a God I wasn't sure I believed in. Paranoid, I closed the curtains in case anyone would see me. I broke down, crying and begging for help. I was desperate. Deep down, I didn't want to die. I wanted to live and be a mum to my beautiful daughter.

From that moment on, I didn't touch a drop of alcohol. I attended AA every evening and at weekends. There were good days and bad days. There were days I could barely move, tearful and consumed with depression.

But it was the beginning of my new way of life. I focused on being there for my daughter as much as I could, driving her to school and being there for her at home-time. No matter what was going on in my life, I made sure I got to my AA meetings.

There were some members of my family who hated me. They kept phoning Social Services on me even though I hadn't lifted a drink. The Social Services would turn up at my door and after chatting to me for a while, they knew I was sober.

I asked a Social Worker: "What can I do, to prove I haven't touched the stuff?"

I even went to my doctor to ask for a blood test to prove my innocence. But they didn't offer that service. So I had to suck it up and get on with it.

My brother's wife has hated me from the first day we met. My drinking problems gave her ammunition to vent her disgust. My brother, meanwhile, who I love dearly, will always be my brother. I've had to accept that his wife put a wedge between us.

I forgive my brother and I forgive myself for letting things get so bad. Given the opportunity, I would still speak to my brother. For me, the bond between siblings can't be broken, no matter what happens. On the other hand, his wife means nothing to me. However, I do wish her all the best for her journey ahead.

Social Services finally signed my case off. Initially, I was allowed to have my daughter overnight, and then eventually, back home. By that stage, I had a good amount of sobriety time under my belt. I vowed to do everything in my power to hold on to it.

CHAPTER EIGHT
Breakthrough in Recovery

IT WASN'T LONG before my childhood trauma began to rear its ugly head again. I was plagued with nightmares and flashbacks. The shame and dirtiness came back with a vengeance, waking me up in the middle of the night with sweats and paranoia.

I went to AA meetings every chance I could get, using the safe space to talk about how I felt. Meanwhile, I did everything I could for my daughter Eva whilst trying to shield her from how I was truly feeling inside.

One evening, I was sharing at an AA meeting about how I was seeing things and feelings things that weren't actually there. I thought I was going insane. A member came up to me at the end.

He said: "Lee, I think you would benefit from seeing a girl I know who is a Spiritual Medium." He gave me her number. Desperate to understand what was happening to me, I contacted her and booked a reading. By this stage, the craving for alcohol had gone but dark suicidal thoughts had returned. I had no idea that my CPTSD was in full swing. Now that the alcohol wasn't there to numb the trauma, it had been catapulted to the forefront of my mind.

There was one Friday evening, after dropping Eva at her Daddy's, I stopped off at my favourite beach. For hours, I just sat there in the car, staring out the window, contemplating suicide. The scary thing was, this time I was sober, so it wasn't even alcohol fuelled.

Obviously, I didn't take any action that night. The only thing that kept running round and round in my head was my daughter. How could I do this to her? It's so selfish to leave her. All I'd be doing it passing my pain onto her. So, mustering all my strength, I started up the car and drove home.

The day came when I was due to have my reading with the Spiritual Medium. Wearing all black, I drove to the lady's house. Black trackie bottoms and black hoodie; it was as if I was hiding from the world. Not knowing what to expect, I was both excited and nervous at the same time.

As soon as I sat down with the lady, an overwhelming feeling of peace washed over me. She began to relay pieces of information about me that no-one else knew.

I didn't know who, if anyone would come through.

However, she was able to connect with my Grandfather (Papa) who had died of throat cancer when I was only two. Growing up, I had heard all about him.

She was able to relay everything that Papa was disclosing – how he was talking about things that were going on in my life. I had never spoken about Papa to anyone so the fact she was able to pass all this on confirmed that it was him.

The lady told me that Papa was saying: "I know what happened to you. If I was still there, things would've been different. I would have stopped it."

I listened in utter shock. In that moment, I felt completely validated. It was an incredible relief.

The medium was also able to connect with Alan, the boy who kissed me in primary school. She described him perfectly; his personality and what he looked like. She also described the unfortunate way in which he died and how long it had been since his passing. Again, I was completely blown away. How was she able to do it?

Alan's message to me was clear: he knew I was in a dark place and that I was thinking of ending things. He implored me not to do it. When he died, he looked back on his life and could see how loved he was. If he could just go back and change his actions on that fatal night, he would have made a different decision. However, he did say that thankfully now, he was in a place of peace.

And then, just like that, he was whistling and back to his usual jokey self. He loved to whistle.

Alan told me that he's been with me all along and is now my spirit guide. He told me that he's protecting me; that the signs I had been receiving were from him.

He also told me that the dreams I had been having were dream visits from him. I had been having the same dream over and over. The scenario may have been different but the message was always the same. In the dream, Alan would appear, smiling and contented. I was so happy to see him and I would wake up with an intense feeling of peace and love.

At first, he appeared in my dreams standing off in the distance. As time went on, he came closer and appeared clearer. Eventually he stood right in front of me, talking but never moving his mouth. It was telepathy; mind-to-mind.

The medium and I are still good friends to this day. We keep in touch and see each other on various occasions. She helped me so much with the spiritual side of things and has been a fundamental part in my next chapter of my life.

A truly beautiful soul. She is my earth angel. My soul sister.

One evening, I really didn't feel like going but I was forcing myself to get ready for an AA meeting. Getting dressed, I put the radio on. The song: "See you again," by Wiz Khalifa and Charlie Puth was playing.

The words of the song hit me to my core. Alan immediately came into my mind. A strong tingling feeling spread all over my body, stopping me in my tracks. The most beautiful wave of love surrounded me in that moment.

The feeling was like standing in an icy cold snow-covered forest, when suddenly a blazing fire lights up in front of you warming your skin. Appearing in front of you is someone you have longed to see again.

I have immense gratitude for Alan, for choosing to be my guiding light.

This is the first time I have shared this experience with anyone. With Alan's permission from spirit side, he is happy for me to share this with you. He also wants to pass on this message to you:

Your life is worth living. Your struggles do not define you. The shadows of life may feel overbearing but please know your life is precious. You are so loved. You are being guided to walk your path and face your struggles. Ask for help. Know that you are deserving of support no matter what you are going through. Choose to fight on, one little step at a time.

What was even more surprising, was that the medium told me she could see gifts in me. She could see that I was a Spiritual Medium just like her. She knew that I was able to see, hear and feel spirit.

Aha! So I wasn't going insane! I thought.

That whole reading changed my life. Not only did it change my view of the world, but also my perception of myself and my experiences.

I drove away from that reading, smiling and crying in the car. It was as though she had switched on a light within me and lifted the black cloud. Knowing I had support from spirit set me on a completely new path.

Filled with a thirst for knowledge, I started to research everything about being a Medium. I watched YouTube videos and read books. I learned so much and began connecting with spirit people through prayer and meditation.

My spirit people became an integral part of my sobriety. I found strength in my Higher Power, Papa and Alan.

I attended a spiritual church every week, learning how to tap into my abilities. Eventually, in my own time, I was able to do platform mediumship and one-to-one readings.

I was desperate to give back and help others who were struggling with life.

Between AA and my Higher Power, I started to change the way I was living. I still struggled with CPTSD but I persevered. On the nights I struggled to get to an AA meeting, all of a sudden, I'd feel a wave of love and warmth wash over me. Because I'm sensitive to energy of spirit, I can feel when spirit is entering my space.

I remember the first time I could feel my Papa in Spirit standing beside me. I could hear him say: "Come on, you can do it! Stand up. Straighten your back. Keep your head held high."

Mum told me that Papa always used to

walk tall. He was a proud man. Immediately, I felt my back straighten.

My spirit was carrying me.

CHAPTER NINE
Time to Face My Trauma

F.E.A.R. = Face Everything and Recover

This saying was often repeated at AA meetings and it always stood out to me. It propelled me to reach for the courage to begin my healing journey to freedom.

The first step of facing everything was finding the strength to report my abuse to the police. I didn't know where it was going to lead, but I knew I had to make that first phone call.

The decision to take action came after watching an item on the local news. A girl had broken her anonymity to talk about her childhood abuse. She spoke about how she was facing this trauma later in life by reporting it to the police. Her bravery subsequently resulted in being able to take her perpetrator to court.

While watching her story, I felt a strong tingling sensation from head to toe; a sign that something is significant and true.

At that moment, I knew I had to contact the police. I didn't talk it over with anyone first of all; I just lifted the phone there and then. It was my first contact with the authorities. I knew, deep in my heart, that this was the road I had to go down in order to heal and recover. I knew I had to address the root cause of my addiction.

It was arranged for me to visit the local police station several days later to make a formal statement. I was terrified. After all, this was completely foreign to me.

I remember walking into the station that day. The room they took me to was tiny; white walls, a table and two chairs. A tape recorder sat on the table. The policeman was very kind and explained the procedure to me in great detail.

I gave my statement, starting the process.

I recalled uncomfortable memories, telling them everything. The only thing I left out was the situation with my cousin. In hindsight, I can see I had totally blocked this out of my mind.

I was told that it would be a long road, but that they would keep me informed every step of the way.

That was in October. It wasn't until the following January that they brought George in for questioning. I received a phone call to say that this had taken place.

He was asked if he knew me. Apparently, he replied: "Yes."

They told him about the allegations against him.

"Did this take place?" They asked him.

He denied everything, which I knew he would do.

The police then put my case forward to the PPS (Public Prosecutions Service). This was a lengthy process. By this stage I had told my parents of what I was doing. To be honest, there really wasn't much response.

Mum said: "Do what you need to do to move on."

When I told Dad about what happened, he was furious. He was fuming that no-one told him at the time. If he knew what had happened, he "would have put him in hospital." Dad was from that generation where "men don't talk about feelings." They just fight it out instead.

My brothers didn't give me any support whatsoever. The support I did receive came from AA and my own Spirit People. Mum supported me when it came to looking after Eva, but there really wasn't any emotional support.

I got relief in AA by venting my emotions in a safe environment. I'm sure some people were thinking: "Here she goes again," but I was always told: "Get it out. Don't leave a meeting until you've shared what's on your mind."

In my mind, my alcoholism stemmed from the childhood abuse, so I needed to vent it in order to stay sober. I didn't give a rat's arse what people thought.

I tended to avoid the women in AA. I

didn't trust women, the reason for which I was to understand later on. It was because of my mum.

I clung onto a few good people in AA who kept me right. I loved going to meetings with them. One person who'll always be in my heart is a guy called Clifford. He was a character. When he walked into the rooms of AA, he had an aura of confidence and determination. I could have listened to him all night. To me, he spoke with truth and tough love. I just really related to him. He took me under his wing and I used to go for coffee with him. I called him my 'AA Dad'.

He actually met my dad one day. They got on really well, chatting about their favourite topic: cars. Clifford loved his cars. He would pick me up for a meeting in his Aston Martin; dark royal blue and beautifully kept. Getting out of the car was a pain in the arse. The best way to get out of the car was to roll out. No kidding.

He always called me "Kiddo". We even went to the gym together for a while. AA members thought we were an item but our friendship was totally platonic.

He never minced his words with me. I loved him like my own dad.

Anyone who has been instrumental in my life, I've carried their golden nuggets of wisdom. In times of struggle, those wise words have carried me through.

One day, I had been struggling and I spoke

to Clifford about it. We were sitting in his kitchen. His home was beautiful; very clean. We sat at a white table, coffee in one hand, cigarette in the other.

Clifford's advice was: "Kiddo, in sobriety you can do anything. You can face anything. Keep your head up and face the fear."

That's exactly what I did.

Even sitting in AA meetings, I could feel spirit around me. One evening, I kept getting the strongest feeling that something had happened to Clifford, but I couldn't pinpoint it.

Clifford? Nah, it couldn't be, I thought, brushing it off.

I couldn't talk to anyone about it because they'd think it was too bizarre.

The tragic day arrived when I got the news that Clifford had passed away.

To make matters worse, prior to his passing, we had fallen out.

He had suddenly cut me off when he got a girlfriend. I felt like I'd done something wrong because he completely ignored me at meetings. I discovered later, that his girlfriend was jealous of our friendship.

The last time I saw him was one week before he died. He was sitting in an AA meeting, looking particularly fragile. He had relapsed, hitting the drink over and over again. Noticing how weak he looked, all I wanted to do was go over and give him a hug.

During his relapse, I had received a phone

call from him. He told me he was sorry for the way he acted. He confided that he had lifted a drink after a long period of sobriety.

I was dumbfounded.

I tried my best to help him get back to AA meetings. He even let me drive one of his cars to a meeting. It was a spanking, clean, black-as-yer-boot Mercedes. He couldn't drive because he still had alcohol in his system, so he handed the keys to me.

Driving along a coastal road on that sunny evening, he told me to put the boot down. I did and boy, it felt amazing!

Clifford was just sitting there, smiling to himself.

There wasn't another car on the road. By the time I got up to 90 mph, the back of the car started to wobble. I slowed down to get her back under control.

Clifford said: "Tell this story to everyone, kiddo, but wait until I'm gone."

I continued to take him to AA meetings, but unfortunately he kept relapsing.

I checked in on him regularly, but he was just sitting there in the dark, Vodka in hand, staring out the window.

Then the news came through. A member of AA announced in the meeting that he had died.

I held it together whilst sitting in the meeting, but afterwards I kept replaying our last few times together: our fall out, his relapse, watching him waste away. It was horrendous to watch someone go through the darkness of alcoholism.

I didn't get to say goodbye. I held onto guilt for all the arguments we'd had.

I don't think you ever really get over the loss of someone. But somehow you find a way to carry them in your heart by remembering the good times and what they meant to you.

Some people come into your life for a reason: to help, support, guide or teach us.

People come and go. Some stay a little longer. While in your life, they may impart wisdom that can help you on your journey.

Clifford's spirit lives on. I know he's around me often, giving me the kick up the arse I need.

CHAPTER TEN
Pandora's Box

AFTER CLIFFORD'S PASSING, I had to put one foot in front of the other. Life went on.

Meanwhile, I was still waiting patiently to hear any updates from the police in relation to my case.

I went to the doctor and explained that I was having flashbacks about the past. I talked about how I had been to the police and reported the abuse. Though courageous, it seemed that opening this can of worms to the authorities was having an adverse effect on me.

The doctor referred me to a psychiatrist, who evaluated me for Post-Traumatic Stress Disorder (PTSD). In some way, receiving the diagnosis was a relief. At least I was finally able to put a label on how I was feeling.

I was also referred to counselling. In fact, I ended up being in therapy for 6 years. Of those 6 years, I went to 3 different therapists until I found the right one for me. I learnt a lot about myself during that time; some stuff I didn't like and some stuff was eye-opening.

There were many "light-bulb moments";

when insights from the therapist would suddenly help me to see why I acted the way I did. I delved into the whole process of working on myself. It was tough, but I was determined. I began to unravel the confusion from my past and come to terms with my issues.

As much as it was a struggle, I also learned a lot about myself. I found out that I wasn't the disgusting, low-life piece of crap that I thought I was. Therapy was a blessing in disguise. I began to like myself.

I started to feel empathy towards myself and others; even the people who hadn't supported me. I started to see the bigger picture.

I began reading about PTSD, which led to falling down a rabbit hole of research. It was painfully fascinating to discover how trauma affected the brain and nervous system. I travelled to events held by inspirational people who had been through trauma and were teaching people like me.

Knowledge is key.

Knowledge is freedom.

I had a deep yearning to understand myself. For me, it wasn't enough to just accept I was traumatised or alcoholic. There was more to my story. I was on a path of healing. When I looked in the mirror, the physical Lee looked back at me, but I knew there was another part bursting to be free.

Through my spiritual work, I was able to delve deep into my subconscious mind. I analysed everything that arose within me. My spiritual side became the foundation for keeping me sober.

AA helped me to get sober, but my faith enabled me to stay sober.

CHAPTER ELEVEN
Surprise Flashback

LIFE WAS BUMBLING along fine. My daughter Eva was doing well, we had moved house and I had maintained my sanity. Until one warm summer's day, that is.

I had just dropped Eva to Play-School at the Community Centre. Walking out of the main doors, I bumped into my Aunt Susan who worked at the centre.

"Hello! How are you doing?"

We stood and chatted, having a friendly catch-up.

Then she asked: "And how are you doing about *the other thing*?"

By her lowered tone and widening of her eyes, I presumed she was asking about my sobriety and how I was getting on in AA.

"Yeah! I'm all good!" I reassured her cheerily. I told her that if I was in much better place.

"No…" Susan began. "How are you doing about *the other thing* – about that incident in the store with George and your cousin?"

I took a step back, my mind reeling. All of a sudden, my thoughts went straight to that day in the store, as though I had been catapulted back in time to that exact spot. It replayed word for word in my head, throwing me completely off balance.

Although trying to regain my composure, I blurted out: "WHAT?! How did you know about that?"

I had never told anyone about it. In fact, I had entirely forgotten about that particular incident until she asked me about it. I had obviously completely blanked it out of my memory.

Susan's eyes widened, realising what she had just unleashed. "Holy shit, Lee." She lowered her head, concern etched on her face. "We need to talk."

"Okay..."

"I think you need to ask your mum about that day in the store, about what happened afterwards. She'll explain everything to you."

"Okay..." I said again, confusion and shock leaving me speechless.

Before we parted ways, she said: "Lee, please know, Robert and I thought that the situation had been taken care of. Once your mum had been told, we thought that was it. There was no mention of it after that."

Susan looked as if she was about to collapse with shock. Meanwhile, my mind simply couldn't process what I was hearing.

I drove to my mum's house, my heart hammering in my chest. Walking in through the front door, I could see that mum was in the kitchen. I called out to her, asking her to come into the living room; that I needed to talk.

In the lounge, we sat opposite each other on brown leather chairs. I repeated what Susan had just told me. I replayed my memory of that day in the store; when she'd announced that my cousin wouldn't be coming to stay anymore.

"Mum," I began. "Did you know I was being abused by George?"

Silence.

"Susan said you knew about it."

Again, silence.

Then she jumped off the chair and walked out of the room, crying.

I followed her into the kitchen.

"Did you know?" I persisted, my voice stubborn now.

She was crying hysterically. All she could say was: "I can't take this anymore! I can't take this anymore!"

She reached into the cupboard looking for tablets.

Time stood still.

I tried to make sense of her reaction.

A wave of sickness washed over me.

She knew rightly what I was asking her.

Eventually, she responded.

"I didn't know," she said quietly.

But she looked like a rabbit caught in the headlights.

I couldn't get anything else out of her. The

only thing she could say was that she didn't know anything. She said that Aunt Susan and Uncle Robert were lying.

"Fine," I retorted. "I'm going up to see them tonight, so I'll hear their side."

My mind raced. Baffled and shocked, it made me question everything I thought I knew about my family.

That evening, I went and knocked on Aunt Susan's door. Opening the door, she welcomed me in and led me to the kitchen where she made us both a coffee. Uncle Robert was there too.

Susan and Robert began to tell me their side of the story.

They were young at the time, in their early 20's. They had gone up to visit Robert's mum, who was my Nan. They were chatting in the kitchen when all of sudden, they heard a crashing sound. My other aunt stormed out of the living-room door, crying hysterically.

Robert and Susan ran over to her to see what was wrong.

Aunt Edna blurted out about her son Charlie; that he had told her about an incident in the store room with Lee and George. Her face like thunder, she announced that Charlie won't be coming back to stay ever again.

Uncle Robert rang his brother, who was Charlie's Dad.

"Get up here now so we can find the bastard!"

Robert wanted to go and kick the living

daylights out of George, but my Uncle Bob had other ideas.

"No," was his response. He didn't want anything to do with it and he didn't want to get involved.

Robert flew down to George's house, ready to do battle on his own. Susan shouted after him, begging him not to go. She was terrified of the damage he'd do.

Robert hammered on George's door, adrenaline flooding through him.

No answer.

George wasn't in.

Was this Divine intervention?

I do believe Robert was being looked after by the powers that be. Robert was so angry that God knows what would've happened if he'd got his hands on George.

Robert trudged back up to Nan's house. Robert and Susan phoned my mum and asked her to come up to the house. They then proceeded to tell her what happened.

Mum's response was: "What do you expect me to do? I needed a babysitter."

My aunt and uncle assumed that mum would tell dad who would then report it to the police.

But that wasn't the case.

Instead, George was asked to come back to babysit me again.

Meanwhile, Robert and Susan assumed the matter had been dealt with.

I listened to Robert and Susan's side of the

story while they listened to the abuse I suffered. There wasn't even anger; just a numb nothingness. I couldn't process their words. How could my mum have sent me back there, into the lion's den?

Susan and Robert were profusely sorry for not reporting it. They wanted to be able to intervene more, but they had been told that the situation was being dealt with.

"It's okay," I told them. After all, it was my parents' responsibility to deal with it, not theirs.

From that moment on, Robert and Susan were stuck to my side like glue. They stood by me every step of the way. I knew I'd have to go back to the police and report this latest development. Robert and Susan assured me they would give their statements when the time came.

We hugged and I headed towards my car. I opened the driver's door and sat behind the wheel. I just sat there, blank, not yet starting the engine. My mind had been shocked into emptiness. It was as though I was catapulted to an old western scene in a movie, where the town is deserted and there isn't a soul in sight; as though the wind was howling ferociously and tumbleweed was spiralling past.

I was right back in the void again. My life fell down around me. It was as though I was standing in that metaphorical deserted field again. This time, there was only darkness. The silence deafened me.

Arriving home, I caught a reflection of myself in the mirror. Emptiness stared back at me. There was nothing. As I knew it, my life had ended. My world, my perception of me, my view of the people who were meant to protect me, shattered like a glass breaking into smithereens.

I cried for hours, replaying everything in my mind. I wanted to escape but I knew I couldn't. I knew I couldn't drink again. I wanted to self-harm; to unleash some of the pain. But that little voice inside me whispered: "Lee, you have Eva. You have to be strong for her".

Swallowing my grief, I went to check on Eva who was in bed sleeping.

Then, standing at the front door, I lit cigarette after cigarette, looking up at the sky while smoking my brains out.

Susan's words popped into my mind: "Lee, it's sink or swim. What's it going to be?"

Stubbing a cigarette out, I chose to swim.

✶

I WRITE THIS part of my story, not to blame or shame anyone, only to speak my truth.

I've accepted I won't get the answers I need from my mum. I had to find a way to separate that from the natural bond I have with her. Whatever her reason was, she didn't help when I needed her the most.

Whilst I thankfully had the love and support from my Uncle Robert and Aunt Susan, there were other members of the extended family who turned their backs on me. I will never understand how they chose not to deal with what was happening, to bury their heads in the sand and ignore the fact that a child was being abused. There's too much hurt there, which prevents me for forgiving family who deserted me when they should have been protecting me. Personally, I don't know how they can live with it on their conscience. If I knew of any child being abused, I'd be marching straight to the authorities and defending the innocent youngster who can't defend themselves.

As I say, the hurt prevents me from understanding. All I know is that there will come a day when they will have to look back on their lives. They will have to remember and they will have to ask themselves: "Why?"

CHAPTER TWELVE
Fighting for the Truth

I TRIED TO talk to my mum about the abuse on numerous occasions. Every single time, I kept getting the same response: "I wasn't told about this."

My aunt and uncle were called liars many times, but my gut feeling was that it was my mum who was lying. It was agony.

Every single time I recounted my memories to her, it only ended up in an argument. Every single time, I got more and more distressed. I was searching for answers but getting nowhere. I just kept hitting a brick wall.

The only thing I could do was vent at my AA meetings. It was there that I was found some relief and support.

Every time I spoke to my dad about it, he said: "Lee, if I'd have known about it, I'd have put him in hospital. He'd only be able to drink through a straw".

There was a distinct difference in feeling between my mum and dad. In my gut, I knew who was telling the truth.

I then decided to phone my cousin. I asked him if he remembered the incident in the store.

He said no.

I didn't know if he did remember but just didn't want to be involved. Perhaps he didn't remember because he was younger than me. Regardless, I had to accept his answer.

I told him about how I had reported the incident to the police. Of course, he already knew this via Aunt Edna and Uncle Bob. Mum had been filling them in on everything.

By this stage, everyone in the extended family knew about the incident. Apparently, there were family members who had plenty to say about it, especially behind my back.

An AA member was very kind to come with me for my second police interview. I had to speak in front of a camera which was nerve-wrecking, not to mention the pain of having to retell the flashback.

Halfway through the interview, I was allowed outside for a smoke break. Standing in the car park, my mobile rang.

"Hello?"

Immediately, I knew by the tone of voice, it was Social Services.

Apparently a family member had phoned to tell them I'd been drinking again.

I hadn't.

The Social Services said that they'd be coming to my house, which was fine by me because I had nothing to hide.

Seriously! I thought. What do these people want from me? I'm just trying to sort my life out; to stay sober and be a good mum.

"You're going to bring shame on the family," one member of the extended family said.

Hearing the word "shame" made me feel worthless; like shit on a shoe. It was as though they were picking at a scab, re-triggering old trauma. All I wanted to do was cry, but I fought back the tears.

A child shouldn't be made to bear the burden of shame. Yet when a perpetrator abuses a child, it's the child who ends up carrying the shame. A child can't make sense of this shame. When a child's sexuality is awakened early, it's confusing. I had no idea about sex. The feelings were alien to me. My body was reacting to touch without my consent. It was mixed signals; my body hurt, my mind was confused.

A child should be carefree and playful while growing up, not living in fear and under control. A child shouldn't have to process such adult stuff at such a young age.

A child should be allowed to hold onto their innocence and grow at their own pace.

Abuse leaves a heavy burden on children; physically, emotionally and mentally.

It seemed that people wanted me to fail. They presumed I'd succumb to alcohol and end up losing my daughter. They were trying to break me down.

However, even in the face of all that, I kept my head up. Social Services didn't pursue me. There was no way I was going to quit now. I had come too far.

Sink or swim, Lee. What do you choose?

Even after the call from the Social Services that day, I gathered myself together and carried on with the interview.

The police had contacted my other aunt and uncle, but they didn't want to get involved. However, they could be summoned if the Public Prosecution took my case to trial. Mum and Dad could be summoned too.

I discovered which family member had phoned the Social Services to report me. I even went to the trouble of contacting NSPCC. This was where the call first came in before it was transferred to Social Services. I received the recording of that first call and the moment I heard the voice, I knew who it was reporting me.

It was no surprise. *To hell with them!* I thought.

Eventually, I had to cut myself off from all of my family except for dad.

Along with my daughter, I kept myself to myself. Eva didn't ask any questions. She was in her own little bubble, shielded from what was going on. A happy little camper.

I moved out of my home town, away from the negativity. I lived by the coastline where it was quiet and beautiful. It was such a relief. I spent many days walking along the beach and exploring country sides and forests. I craved peace.

I kept my life as quiet as possible. There were days when I didn't want to get out of bed. On the days that Eva was in school, I attended counselling. I found healthier ways of coping.

Meanwhile, I was waiting to hear if my case was going to court. It was a long wait; nearly two years from when I first went to the police.

Initially, I tried to maintain a relationship with mum but I kept getting triggered every time I saw her. It was preventing me from finding any healing or peace. I had to accept that, as much as I loved my mum and family, I had to cut ties for my own sanity. Denial can't exist when you're fighting for the truth.

CHAPTER THIRTEEN
Court Week

THE DAY FINALLY arrived when I received the letter from the PPS. With trembling hands, I read how they would be pursuing my case. It would commence later that year.

Relief swept over me. The PPS felt that my case was worthy enough to be pursued. Finally, after all the heartache and searching, I felt validated and heard.

It's a shame I had to seek that validation from counsellors and the police. Deep down, I had wanted the support from my family, but hell would freeze over before they would acknowledge the abuse.

Fortunately, I did have the support from my aunt and uncle and they went to the court house with me to meet the barrister.

On arrival, she led us into the room where my trial would take place the following week. She wanted me to get a feel for the court and be mentally prepared. She asked me to get up into the witness stand which gave me a glimpse of what it would look like on the day.

She even asked me dummy questions, prepping me with the kind of inquisition I should expect from the opposing side. She warned me that the Defence would try to rip me to shreds. They would likely use my alcoholism against me, painting me as a bad mother. They would try their best to trip me up. I nodded, taking in all her advice. All I could do was tell the truth.

Thankfully, George and I would be in separate rooms for the trial. I wouldn't see him on arrival, but I might bump into him at some stage.

After an anxiously long week, the morning of the Court date finally arrived. It was a Monday morning and Susan, Robert and I travelled down together. We stopped off at a petrol station on the way for a coffee. Standing beside the car, drinking our coffees and having a smoke, there wasn't much chat out of us. The anxiety had really kicked in.

Arriving at the Court, we parked the car and took the terrifying walk to the Court entrance. Mechanically, we made our way through security where they checked our bags and walked us through the security scanner. We were led down to a room which had been allocated to us. My mum and stepdad arrived, as did my dad.

My ex-husband arrived also. Not only did he want to support me, but there was also a chance he could be called to the stand. I had confided to him during our marriage about what had happened to me as a child, so they might have needed him to clarify the details.

My other aunt and uncle didn't turn up, but they could have been summoned at any time during the trial.

There was a sofa and chairs in the room, as well as a tea and coffee machine. We were told to help ourselves.

Then the barrister turned up, sweeping into the room. Holding a large file, she was wearing a black cloak and cream tie wig. Her professional appearance suddenly made me feel completely out of my comfort zone.

Then she issued the bad news. She said that there was another case which might take precedence over mine. Apparently this other case had been put off time and time again. If that case was heard this week, my case could be postponed until the following year!

My heart sank. Even though I was full of nerves and adrenaline, the thought that it could be postponed made me sick to my stomach. I'd been waiting long enough.

However, I just smiled and said: "Okay."

She asked us all to wait while she went and clarified things. We all sat there in the room in awkward silence. My Mum and stepdad sat further away from me, my aunt and uncle. Dad was trying to make small talk but the atmosphere was thick with tension. Sitting on one side of the room was my aunt and uncle, who had been called liars by my mum and stepdad. On the other side was mum who looked terrified.

The anxiety made me go right up into my

head, anxious thoughts swirling around my mind. All I could do was pray to my Papa.

Please let my case be heard today. I can't do this anymore. I can't wait any longer.

I really needed this case to be over and done with. I felt as if it was holding me back. Pleading with my spirit people, I repeated the words over and over in my mind: *Please let this happen today. Please let my case be heard. Please.*

Nausea rose up inside me. I felt sick.

I knew that if the case didn't go ahead, I would drink again. I had stayed strong all this time, waiting for this moment. If I was told it wouldn't continue, it would crush me. The thought of alcohol was heavy on my mind.

Time dragged. It was absolute torture waiting for the barrister to come back.

Then, all of a sudden, I started to feel a tingling sensation. Goosebumps formed all over my body. A voice in my mind said: It's okay. It's going to be ok.

It was my Papa.

Eventually, the barrister arrived back. She announced that she needed to speak to me in private. I asked my Uncle Robert to come with me because I knew I'd struggle to retain any information. It was all too overwhelming.

It's okay. It's going to be okay. My Papa had said.

But how was this going to be okay?

Then, what I heard next completely blew my mind.

I must have checked out, mentally left the building, brain switched off.

Because I certainly wasn't expecting what came next.

CHAPTER FOURTEEN
Turn of Events

"LEEANNE, THERE'S BEEN a development," the barrister sat opposite me while Uncle Robert and I listened intently.

"It's up to you what you want to do, but George wants to plead guilty."

My face must have had a shocked zoned-out expression because she repeated herself.

"Did you hear me Leeanne? George wants to plead guilty!"

My uncle nudged me, repeating the barrister's words.

It took a moment, trying to digest what she was saying.

"What does that mean? What will happen now?" I asked.

"Well," she began, "It means that he is taking responsibility for what he did to you."

"So what now happens now?" Uncle Robert repeated.

"Well, you have two options," she explained. She advised that if I declined George's guilty plea, I would have to wait until the following year for a trial. If I accepted, the whole case would be over and done with that day.

"I want to wait for the trial," I blurted out.

Uncle Robert looked at me quizzically, but in my mind, I wasn't going to let George get away with it. Why should he get to walk out of Court without any questioning? And what about all those people who called my aunt and uncle "liars". I wanted them to hear the truth. Family members had dismissed me, didn't listen to me or even acknowledge what had happened to me. I wanted to have my day in court – for them to hear what really happened.

"Why don't you go, have a coffee and think about it", the barrister advised. "You don't even need to make your decision today."

Robert and I went outside to have a smoke. We walked through the big black entrance gates. It was a beautiful day.

Robert was ecstatic but trying to stay calm. He went through everything the barrister had said and explained my options again.

I was adamant I wanted a trial.

"They're getting away with it, Robert. I can't let them win."

"No. They haven't won, Lee," Uncle Robert said firmly. "Lee, you've won. You've won! That bastard has just pleaded guilty! You have won, Lee!"

Uncle Robert also advised me that if I waited another year for the trial, it would only bring more pain. As well as that, the trial could go either way. What if he was found not guilty by a jury?"

I listened, my mind struggling.

"Lee," Robert went on excitedly, "all those people doubted you. By George admitting what he did, it's proving you were telling the truth. You can walk away with your head held high."

Deep down in my heart, I knew he was right. I knew I had to accept George's plea and get it over with. It was the end of the line. I didn't have the strength to fight anymore. I was done, emotionally and mentally. The ramifications had been detrimental to my health. Alcohol was lurking in my mind. I couldn't risk my life or my daughter any longer.

I decided to accept George's plea.

Robert and I headed back to the room where everyone else was waiting. They were itching to find out what was going on.

The barrister took us aside again. I told her I would accept his plea.

"In all the years of practising law, this has never happened…" the barrister admitted. "…someone pleading guilty just before a trial."

This gave me comfort. Now I knew why my spirit people were telling me it was going to be okay.

We went back into the room where the others were waiting. The barrister announced my decision.

Then everyone in our group was led down into the court room. It was very small and smelt of old wood.

Robert, Susan and I were sitting close to the box where George would be standing.

Everyone got into position; my barrister, our group and George's defence.

It seemed as though we were waiting for ages. Then we heard: "All rise."

It was very intimidating.

The Judge arrived and sat in his chair. After some introductions, he called for George to enter the room. Someone went to a side door and ushered George to stand in the box. He was asked to give his name. The Judge read out the charges and asked if he understood what he was being charged with.

Looking at George didn't bring up any emotions for me. I felt nothing. There was neither anger nor fear. All I could see was a very old man who looked pitifully frail and sick.

George pleaded guilty. The judge announced that sentencing would take place in Newtownards courthouse the following Thursday.

Outside the Court, I stood with Robert and Susan, having a smoke and trying to digest the surprise turn of events. We had been pumped up with adrenaline, ready for the first day of trial, to then be told it might not go ahead, to George then pleading guilty. It was one hell of a day.

Now it would be another wait to hear what his sentencing would be.

To be honest, I just wanted to be validated.

I knew there was a chance of George going to prison. I knew that if my mum and others were called to the witness stand, it would have an impact on them. I wanted them to be questioned.

However, with the turn of events, it meant they had evaded the stand. They had dodged being thrown questions at them by my barrister. That's all I ever wanted; for them to acknowledge what had happened to me.

CHAPTER FIFTEEN
Retribution

IT WASN'T LONG before we were heading back to Court, this time to hear the sentencing. Unlike the previous time, when I had been full of nerves and adrenaline, this time, I was strangely calm.

After dropping Eva at school, I went home and took my time getting ready. I was due to be at Court by 10.30am. Loyal as ever, Robert and Susan met me outside the courthouse.

On arriving at Court, a journalist from the local newspaper greeted me.

I had contacted the paper and asked them if they would like to cover my story.

My reason? I wanted to get my story out there, to hopefully help someone else. Just I had been inspired when I watched the news item about the woman who broke her anonymity, I hoped to be the same light at the end of the tunnel for someone else.

Steven, the journalist, was very pleasant and calm. He let me know that he would be there throughout the whole court session, recording the sentencing.

Strangely, there were no feelings of fear or

hurt or anger; no concerns about how strict or lenient the sentence would be. I was just relieved. Today would be the end of it. From now on, I could move on with my life.

Reassured by the presence of Robert and Susan, we entered the building together. Although held in Newtownards court this time, it was the exact same process; we were ushered through security, then called into the court room.

"All Rise," the booming voice announced.

Once again, the judge called for George to be brought in. Once again, he was led to the stand, stepping into the box stand.

The judge repeated the charges to him. He announced that, because George made a guilty plea the previous week, the purpose of the court session that day was to conclude punishment.

Then it was the turn of my barrister to make her proposals to the judge, followed by George's defence making their comments.

My barrister stood up, addressing the judge with her confident and assertive manner. She talked about how the abuse had impacted my life, not just at the young age when the incidents took place, but the lasting long-term effects later in life. How I had been diagnosed with CPTSD and how I had turned to addiction as a means of shutting off emotions.

Sitting there listening to her retell my story, it almost felt like I was hearing someone else's unfortunate events. Suddenly, the magnitude of what I had been through really hit home. Holy shit. I have been through the ringer. And yet I'm still standing.

In that moment, there was a sense of compassion for myself, an acknowledgement of all I had overcome. A moment of healing.

Then it was time for George's defence to give their speech.

They talked about the struggles George had faced. How he had suffered from alcoholism throughout his life. In recent times, he had also been diagnosed with an aggressive bowel cancer. It only took one look at him to see how frail, withered and aged he was as a result of the two diseases.

Having attended AA for some time, and having listened to a vast number of alcoholics, I knew the mental torture of alcoholism.

For me, alcoholism resulted in temporarily losing my daughter. Alcoholism ripped me of dignity. It broke me down until I felt nothing but inner hell. It was like a demon sucking my soul.

I had always said I wouldn't wish alcoholism on my worst enemy.

I had heard the phrase: "Hurt people, hurt people." I'd never really understood that phrase before. Until that moment.

Standing there in that court, seeing how weak, frail and pitiful he looked, I could understand his pain. I had felt his pain. I had been in his shoes. I knew what hell felt like.

Strangely, the feelings of anger and hate

were not there that day. Instead, there was a feeling of pity. I'm not sure if pity is the right word, but something in me changed. Perhaps it was understanding. I certainly wasn't condoning his behaviour, but perhaps there was a sense of acceptance. It was a feeling that took me by surprise.

Hurt people, hurt people.

People who hurt re-enact their pain onto other people.

Some hurt people inflict the pain inwards to themselves, but other hurt people act outwards, inflicting their pain on others.

In that moment, sitting in court that day, I felt the tears fall silently down my face. It was a weird feeling of empathy, pity and understanding. This person, who had inflicted so much pain on my life, was in agony too.

When he pleaded guilty that day, it sent a message to those who had doubted me; the family members who had called me a liar. The message said: Stuff you! It's just come out of the horse's mouth: Guilty. There you go, he said it himself!

The time came for the Judge to read out George's sentence.

George was issued a jail sentence for 14 months.

The sentence would be suspended for 3 years.

He was free to go.

I actually wasn't shocked with the sentencing. I was just relieved that it was over. He had pleaded guilty. I could put it behind me.

The judge made his own comments about the sentencing. He said he took George's terminal Bowel Cancer into consideration. George was dying. He was receiving on-going medical treatment but the diagnosis was that he didn't have long to live.

He was placed on the Sex Offender's Register for 10 years; basically for the rest of his life. He was also issued with a Sexual Offences Prevention Order. He'd never be able to harm another child again.

Lifting our coats and bags, we got up and made our way out of the building. My barrister had asked me to wait for her as she wanted to talk to me.

I watched George come out of the Court too. I saw him walking, frail and weak, towards the town centre. The journalist was hot on his heels, snapping pictures of him. His face would be plastered all over the newspaper the following day.

My barrister came over and gave me a hug, congratulating me for being so strong and brave throughout the whole process. The police officer who dealt with my case also came over to give me a hug and say goodbye. I don't know if it was a coincidence but he told me that my case would be his last. He'd be moving on to new pastures.

My aunt and uncle joined me for my interview. We sat on a park bench, where the journalist met us, taking pictures and interviewing me.

That Sunday, my story was in the paper: "Woman hopes to give victims courage to speak out."

The article was very tastefully written, ending with my Uncle's words: "I'm proud of her. Shame on him and shame on anyone who doubted what Leeanne said had happened to her. Justice was done."

Going through the experience of reporting George and taking him to court was extremely difficult for me. I had to face my past all over again.

But it was also very healing and freeing. I started to feel compassion for myself and what I had been through. I had learnt a lot about myself as a result of going to therapy. What I didn't expect, was to feel forgiveness for George.

I received closure that day.

Finally, I was able to take the baggage that George had placed on my young shoulders and hand it firmly back.

CHAPTER SIXTEEN
Acceptance

THROUGHOUT THIS JOURNEY, I have unfortunately learned that not everyone is good for me. That includes family.

My relationship with my mum has shifted. I still love her and I can still be around her, especially when it's with my daughter. However, I've had to put boundaries in place. Emotionally, I can't open up to her the way I used to. I've had to put distance in place for my own wellbeing.

Through the help of therapy and AA, I've learned that I can't engage in drama. For that reason, I've had to distance myself from certain family members. Knowing that they turned their back and didn't believe me doesn't sit well.

I'm the type of person who tries to see the best in people. At times, this was to my own detriment. I was naïve to think that everyone would be friendly and supportive. I used to be the kind of person who would let others say and do anything to me. I even went back for seconds and thirds. Deep down, I thought that people were good at their core. However, the truth is, some people just fester in negativity.

I've had to move away from that negativity. I've had to find my own peace and contentment. I've had to work hard on myself. Today, I value ME. I have a life to live. I put myself first now.

I no longer feel ashamed.

I no longer hate myself.

Today, I respect my boundaries.

Today, I love me for me.

Final Words of Gratitude

I have so much love and respect for Uncle Robert and Aunt Susan. They fought beside me every step of the way. There were so many times they said they "wish they had done more to help me", but I've assured them many times that it wasn't their fault. They were told it was "being handled" so they couldn't have done any more. They helped me to stand up and speak the truth. They made it possible for me to face the challenges of going to court. While I tried to free myself of the heavy burden I'd carried, they were my solid foundation of support. They are forever in my heart.

I feel humbled by the support I received from AA members who listened and encouraged me. They are amazing, like-minded, beautiful souls.

Thank you to my counsellors who listened to me week in, week out, bearing the brunt of my emotions.

Thank you, Darren (Daz) Linton of Recovery & Resilience Coaching for his amazing support. Daz has helped me to move away from addiction and trauma and find balance in my life.

Thank you, Rose McClelland for helping me to make my dream a reality. I wanted to publish my life story in the hope that it will help someone like me.

I also want to acknowledge my Spiritual team and Spirit family for their support. My Spiritual network has been my safety net. Every time I wanted to give up hope, they held me and picked me back up. My Spirit family cannot speak for themselves but I can be their voice. Thank you for all your encouragement, love and support.

Thank you to my Papa – David Simpson, my Grandfather; a proud man indeed.

Thank you to Alan – my forever friend. Kind and charming, who loves to whistle; my guiding light.

Thank you to my dear friend Clifford who left me this golden nugget: "You can do anything in sobriety, kiddo."

Thank you to my Guides, Angels and Spirit family. There are too many to mention but you know I love you all.

Last but not least… Thank you to ME; the childhood Leeanne thanking the adult Leeanne. Thank you for fighting for yourself; for never giving up hope that you could make it through.

One day at a time, I will keep walking and looking up at the STARS.

Starlight

Memories surround her
    as time passes by.
    A lost soul searching in the dark
    just a little girl inside yearning to find a spark.
    A spark of light is all she needed.
    Then out of nowhere as she wandered through the dark
    A light appeared in the night sky stars.
    As she gazed at this light,
    her eyes filled with tears.
    She felt something wonderful within her heart,
    something she had never felt before.
    This feeling lifted the little girl up
    and carried her towards the light.
    As she got closer, she felt herself ask:
    "Who are you?"
    The light replied: "I am part of you, my dear. I am your light."
    "Of me?" the little girl asked, curious. "How?"
    "Well my dear, a long time ago, I wished YOU into existence."
    "You were born a beautiful light, much like these shining stars. You hold starlight in your heart."

"Little one, you hold the key to making your light shine."

The little girl replied: "How can I shine when I'm stuck in the dark? I can't see."

The light replied: "That is why I am here, to show you. Your key can unlock the light within."

"Close your eyes. Search inside your mind. Find a moment in time when you laughed or cuddled your favourite teddy bear."

The little girl did as the light said. She found a memory that made her feel good inside. She shed a tear when she realised how warm the memory made her feel.

The light said: "Now, pick a star in the sky."

The little girl picked a star that shone so bright.

The light carried her to this star.

"Close your eyes and take a deep breath," the light instructed.

Almost in an instant, she felt warm and tingly inside her heart. Even with her eyes closed, she could see the light brighten.

The light said softly: "I am your guiding light. With this star in your heart, we will keep you in the light. I will forever be your guide, walking with you on your journey. There will be times when you enter the darkness. But now that you have the key to your bright light, you'll never be lost in the dark memories of the past. I will hold this space for you."

At that, the light took a place in the night

sky, smiling at her as it drifted upwards.

The little girl said: "Ah! You are me and I am you!" She no longer felt alone in the dark for she knew that the light was within her.

The starlight was her guiding light.

About the Author

Leeanne Truesdale is a Spiritual Psychic Medium, giving Spirit their voice when connecting to loved ones. Leeanne works within the light of Consciousness, bringing guidance, support and connection. Her aim is to help those who face life's struggles. Leeanne also connects deeply on a soul-to-soul level with animals that are put on her path for healing.

Leeanne started her Spiritual journey when her life fell apart. She has always been able to see and sense Spirit but she initially shut it down due to fear and childhood trauma.

Although coming from a dysfunctional background and disempowered throughout her life, Leeanne managed to take back her own power. She chose to face life and heal.

Her journey has been a long road but worth facing. Regardless of how many times she's been knocked down, she always tries to see the light in people.

Today, Leeanne is just an ordinary girl who loves life.

Printed by Amazon Italia Logistica S.r.l.
Torrazza Piemonte (TO), Italy